Mushrooms

by Roger Phillips

assisted by Jacqui Hurst

Elm Tree Books London

INTRODUCTION

Aim

In this book we have aimed to photograph the most common and important mushrooms that are found in the British Isles and Europe.

How to use this book

The gilled mushrooms (Agarics) are arranged in spore colour order, starting with white spores, then cream, then brown, dark brown and black. This is followed by mushrooms with pores (Boletes) and finally, the toothed mushroom (Hydnum). Most mushrooms are shown in their natural habitat, and then again laid out to show the important details. On other spreads related mushrooms are shown for comparison. It must be remembered that this book shows only a part of the vast number of mushrooms and fungi that can be found in Europe.

What is a mushroom?

The mushroom that you see above ground is the spore-producing fruiting body of the mushroom plant which is in the soil, leaf litter, dung, or wood on which the mushroom is found. The plant consists of tiny white, or coloured, strands (mycelium) which run through the material on which the plant lives. Mushrooms do not contain chlorophyll and, therefore, must obtain their necessary carbon compounds from other plants, or in rare cases, animals.

The Photographs

The studio photographs were taken on a Bronica 120 format with a 75mm lens. Scale: ○ is 1cm. The field photographs were taken on a Nikon FM camera with a 50mm lens, occasionally with close-up attachments. The film was Kodak Ektachrome 64 ASA in both cases, but when used outdoors it was pushed one stop in development.

Edible or Poisonous

Only eat those mushrooms that you are sure are edible. Always consult an expert until you are certain of your identification. If you feel any distressing symptoms and there is a possibility of poisoning go to the emergency department of your nearest hospital.

Russula sardonia under Scots Pine

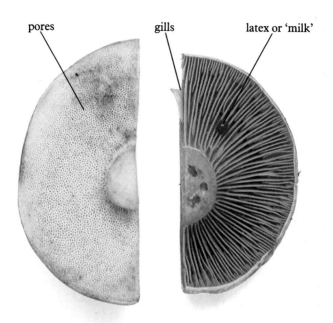

pores   gills   latex or 'milk'

Glossary

amatoxins	deadly poisonous compounds found in some *amanitas*
auto-digest	deliquesce
boss	a raised central area as in shield boss
deliquesce	the gills liquify and gradually disappear
fibrils	a small fibre
gills	spore producing layer in *agarics*
KOH	potassium hydroxide in a 20/40% solution
margin	the edge of a mushroom cap
phallotoxins	poisonous compounds found in *Amanita phalloides*
ring	remains of the partial veil left on the stem
sac	a loose volva at the base of some species from which the mushroom appears to grow
tomentum	a matted covering of hairs
tube	the spore producing layer in *boleti*
umbo	a central lump on a mushroom cap
veil	a protective layer covering or partially covering the young mushroom
volva	cap-like bag enclosing the base of the stem, remains of a universal veil

The Blusher

The Blusher photographed 1 September

The Blusher

Amanita rubescens is one of the most common mushrooms of both deciduous and conifer woodlands throughout Britain. Although the cap colour varies from cream to dark brown there is always a flush of pinky-red in it, especially in damaged areas. The patches of reddish-fawn material on the cap and the swollen base to the stem are also distinctive. This mushroom is **poisonous raw** but can be eaten when well cooked. However, as there are many poisonous mushrooms in the *amanita* group it is much safer to avoid eating it.

Cap 5–15cm across, whitish-yellowish or more commonly brownish-red with patches varying from greyish-white to pinkish. In very wet weather the patches may wash off. **Gills** white, often with brown spots. **Stem** white or reddish with a floppy ring and a swollen base. Season late summer to late autumn.

Caesar's Mushroom photographed 15 August

Caesar's Mushroom

Amanita caesarea has not, as yet, been found in Britain. It occurs in warmer areas of Europe, normally extending north, about as far as the Dordogne, but perhaps if our hot summers continue we might hope to find it. It is included in this book because in Europe it is considered by many to be the most important edible mushroom of all. As the name implies, Caesar's Mushroom has been prized since Roman times. Julius Caesar and Claudius were both potty about it. It is said that Claudius was poisoned by a dish purporting to be this mushroom but some had been substituted with the very deadly Death Cap (p. 14).

Cap starts out as a white sac from which the egg-shaped orange cap pushes forth expanding rapidly to 6 or even 18cm across, becoming a lovely yellowy-orange colour with patches of the white sac still remaining attached to it. **Gills** have a soft egg-yellow tint. **Stem** is yellow with a soft yellow ring which is easily detached. The base is surrounded by a white, loose bag or sac called the volva, most of which will be underground. Season summer to autumn.

A traditional way of cooking this delicacy is to fry them with chopped shallots in best olive oil. When they are cooked, throw a liberal helping of finely chopped garlic and parsley over them, cook for about twenty seconds and serve.

Amanita excelsa

Amanita excelsa, *a button, photographed 2 October*

Amanita excelsa, also called *Amanita spissa*, is fairly common in deciduous or conifer woods throughout Britain. Although it is **said to be edible** it is much better avoided as it can easily be confused with the deadly Panther, *Amanita pantharina* (p. 17). The main differences are as follows: *A. excelsa*, has a brownish-grey cap with grey flat patches on it, a ring with lines from the gills marking it, and no collar on the bulb. *A. pantharina* has a more ochre coloured cap with white raised warts on it, no lines on the ring, and a collar around the top of the bulb.

Cap 6–12cm across, greyish or brownish with pale grey flat patches of veil on the surface. **Gills** white or off-white. **Stem** white above the ring, white with grey scales below, bulbous at base. Season late summer to autumn.

9

False Death Cap

False Death Cap photographed 20 October

False Death Cap

Amanita citrina has a lovely pale lemon tint to the cap, though there is a rarer form with an all white cap. The smell is extremely distinctive, resembling freshly-cut new potatoes. It is common in deciduous woods, mainly those of oak and beech. Although this species is not thought to be poisonous it is **never eaten** because of the disgusting taste and also because of its similarity to the real Death Cap (p. 15). False Death Cap is distinguishable from the real Death Cap, however, by its large bulb at the stem base, while the real Death Cap has a floppy sac.

Cap 4–10cm across, whitish when young but most frequently with a pale lemon yellow tint, loosely covered with flat patches of creamy veil. **Gills** white or creamy. **Stem** white with a ring and a large basal bulb with an overturned lip on the top surface. Season late summer and autumn.

Fly Agaric

Fly Agaric photographed 29 October

Fly Agaric

Amanita muscaria is the most frequently illustrated and most easily recognised of our mushrooms. It is rather common, provided you look in the right habitat, that is under birch trees, in late autumn. Fly Agaric is **deadly poisonous** in large quantities, but in some areas of Lapland and Siberia the dried caps were eaten as an intoxicant, a habit that has died out with the introduction of vodka. It is believed that this is 'soma', the mushroom of divine strength and immortality.

Cap 8–20cm across, bright crimson or orange, covered in white pointed scales when young which eventually may drop or wash off. **Gills** white. **Stem** white with a large white or pale yellowish ring near the top. The basal bulb has two or three lip-like rings on the top. Season autumn or late autumn.

Death Cap

Death Cap photographed 27 October

Death Cap

Amanita phalloides is the **deadly poisonous** mushroom responsible for over 80 per cent of deaths. The poisonous amatoxins and phallotoxins it contains attack the liver and kidneys. The poisoning may be difficult to diagnose as the onset may occur as long as 24 hours after eating it. The first symptoms are prolonged vomiting and diarrhoea, then a slight recovery followed by a relapse. Death Caps are found fairly frequently in beech or oak woods throughout Britain. The green or pale fawnish green of the cap and the distinctive loose sac round the basal bulb are the main distinguishing characteristics.

Cap 4–12cm across, dull pale green or white, sometimes with white veil remnants. **Gills** whitish. **Stem** white, often marked with greenish bands. The basal bulb has a loose white sac (volva) clinging to it. Season late summer to late autumn.

15

Panther Cap photographed 27 October

Destroying Angel photographed 3 September

Panther Cap

Amanita pantherina is **deadly poisonous** and distinguished by its pale brown ochre cap with white pyramidal warts and neat collar round the bulb at the stem base. It is found in deciduous woods mainly of oak or beech. **Cap** 6–10cm across, light ochre brown with pure white pointed warts and striate margin. **Gills** white. **Stem** creamy white with a ring and neat round bulb with a distinct collar. Season late summer to autumn.

Destroying Angel, *Amanita virosa*, is a **deadly poisonous**, pure white mushroom found in mixed or deciduous woods. **Cap** 5–11cm across, pure white, conical at first. **Gills** white. **Stem** white with a shaggy fibrous surface and a small bulb with a white, loose sac (volva). Season late summer to autumn. *Amanita verna*, which is very similar, often occurs in spring as well as autumn. The best way to distinguish these two species is with KOH. *A. virosa* instantly turns yellow.

Tawny Grisette

Tawny Grisette photographed 21 September

Tawny Grisette

Amanita fulva is common in mixed or conifer woods and, along with the group of different-coloured *amanitas* similar to it, is distinguished from the previous *amanitas* by the lack of a ring on the stem. It is **edible** although I do not think much of it.

Cap 4–9cm across, light reddish-brown with a striate margin. **Gills** white. **Stem** white or creamy with no bulb at the base but there is a large, loose, floppy, sac-like volva. Season summer to early autumn.

Grisette, *Amanita vaginata*, is also edible and is similar but grey coloured and often larger. *Amanita crocea*, again edible, has a lovely, bright orange cap up to 10cm across, and a stem with a white volva. *Amanita inaurata* is brownish-grey with a stretched out, lumpy ring or rings at the stem base. Its edibility is unknown.

Parasol Mushroom

Parasol Mushroom photographed 7 October

Parasol Mushroom

Lepiota procera is one of the finest mushrooms of all to eat and is found in open woods and on old grassland and heaths. When you find a field with the enormous caps standing well above even tall grass, if you are like me, you will jump for joy.

Cap 10–25cm across when expanded, with a typical parasol shape, the centre forming a point and the edge curving down. The buttons are almost round and do not open quickly so you may often find them at this stage; they are known as drum sticks. The cap is covered with large scales which break up as it expands. **Gills** creamy and soft. **Stem** tall even in the button stage, up to 40cm with a loose ring and distinctive brown scales. Season summer and autumn.

Stinking Baby Parasol

Shaggy Parasol photographed 24 September

Shaggy Parasol

Lepiota rhacodes is similar to the Parasol (p. 21) but not so large. The distinguishing feature is the reddening of the flesh when cut or broken. There is a woodland variety with soft shaggy scales and a variety usually found on garden rubbish heaps with tougher, larger scales. They are both **edible** and good. **Cap** 8–16cm across, cream coloured but covered in brownish scales. **Gills** cream or greyish. **Stem** whitish, bruising reddish, base bulbous. Season summer and autumn.

Stinking Baby Parasol, *Lepiota cristata*, is a small, **inedible** mushroom with a strong acrid smell that is found in woods and on refuse. **Cap** 2–5cm across, conical at first, cream with reddish-brown scales. **Gills** whitish. **Stem** whitish, thin. Season summer to autumn.

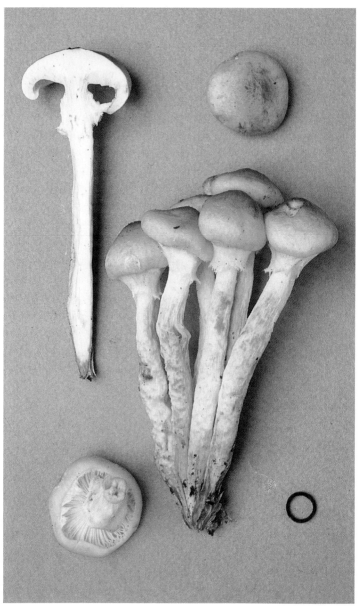

Honey Fungus

Honey Fungus photographed 10 October

Honey Fungus

Armillaria mellea is the scourge of foresters for it is a fungus that destroys trees in large numbers. It is found in big clumps on living or dying trees or growing from the roots nearby. It is a good **edible** fungus when cooked. There are very distinct forms of this mushroom: some with yellow caps and scales, some with reddish-brown caps and scales.

Cap 3–15cm across, yellow, darker in the centre, or yellowish-green or reddish-brown, with small scales. **Gills** creamy. **Stem** white, yellowish or orangy-brown with a large soft ring with either yellow-brown or white scales underneath. The stem bases are sometimes bulbous and often fused together in clumps. Season summer to early winter.

There is a similar species *Armillaria tabescens* that also grows on wood but is distinguishable by its lack of a ring. Edible when cooked.

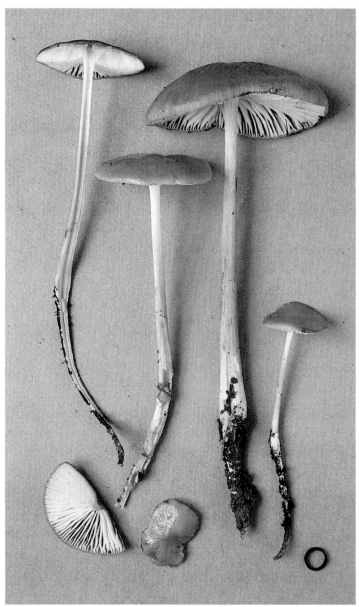

Rooting Shank photographed 3 September

Porcelain Fungus photographed 6 September

Rooting Shank

Oudemansiella radicata is very common in deciduous woods especially beech throughout Britain. The stem goes very deep underground as the mushroom attaches to roots or buried wood. It is too tough to eat. **Cap** 3–9cm across with a raised centre. The surface is deeply wrinkled, light brown in colour. **Gills** pure white. **Stem** white at the top, brown below, deeply rooting and twisted. Season summer to autumn.

Porcelain Fungus, *Oudemansiella mucida*, grows on the trunks of beech trees often quite high up, in clumps. The caps are extremely slimy, but it is **edible** after the slime has been removed. **Cap** 2–8cm across, translucent white or creamish, very slimy. **Gills** white. **Stem** white, getting thicker towards the base with a ring. Season summer to autumn.

St. George's Mushroom

St. George's Mushroom photographed 1 May

St. George's Mushroom

Tricholoma gambosum, as its common name suggests, is a spring mushroom fruiting, legend has it, on 23 April, St. George's Day. In my experience this is a bit early, it usually comes a week or two later. It is a good **edible** mushroom with a strong mealy taste and smell. Personally I don't like to eat the large old specimens, only the young fresh buttons. It is found on old pastures or at woodsides or roadsides in grass and is reasonably common throughout Britain.

Cap 5–15cm across, white, discolouring creamish. **Stem** short, white and thick. **Gills** white or cream and crowded, all parts have a strong mealy smell and taste. Season late April or May.

Tricholoma terreum *photographed 29 October*

Tricholoma sulphureum *photographed 29 October*

Tricholoma terreum is distinguished from the other *tricholomas* by its lack of mealy smell. It is not very common but is most frequently found in conifer woods. The very similar *Tricholoma pardinum* is poisonous. **Cap** 4–7cm across, light to dark grey, felty. **Gills** whitish-grey. **Stem** whitish. Season late summer to autumn. **Edible**.

    Tricholoma cingulatum is pale grey and smaller with a ring. **Edible**. *Tricholoma sejunctum* is yellowish, greeny-grey and smells of meal. **Not edible**, causes nausea. *Tricholoma sulphureum* the 'Gas Agaric' is sulphur yellow all over and gives off a strong smell like gas-tar which can be noticed a few yards away. **Not edible**. *Tricholoma flavovirens* is either yellowish or a bit greenish all over with no special smell. It is a good edible species found mainly under conifers. **Edible**.

Tricholoma fulvum *photographed 29 September*

Tricholoma ustale *photographed 21 September*

Tricholoma fulvum is the most common of our *tricholoma*s but though **edible** it is of poor quality. It is found in deciduous woods throughout Britain, usually with birches, and smells mealy. **Cap** 4–9cm across, brown or reddish-brown. **Gills** yellowish, getting spotted brown with age. **Stem** brownish but the flesh inside the stem is yellow if you cut or split it. Season autumn.

Tricholoma ustale looks like a shiny chestnut. It is found in deciduous woods and is **poisonous**. It has no distinctive smell, but *Tricholoma ustaloids* which looks identical has a strong mealy smell. **Cap** 4–8cm across, chestnut brown, sticky when wet. **Gills** whitish, edges blackening with age. **Stem** reddish-brown. Season late summer to autumn.

Plums and Custard photographed 12 September

Tricholomopsis platyphylla *photographed 25 August*

Plums and Custard

Tricholomopsis rutilans is commonly found growing on old conifer stumps throughout Britain. It is said to be **edible** but I don't recommend it. **Cap** 4–12cm across, covered in dense, plum-coloured scales, and yellow underneath. **Gills** a lovely egg-yolk yellow. **Stems** yellowish, covered in purple scales. Season late summer to late autumn.

Tricholomopsis platyphylla is distinguished by having long, white, root-like strands running from the stem base to the buried wood stumps or beech husks on which it grows. It has a bitter taste and is **not edible**. Common in deciduous woods, especially beech, throughout Britain. **Cap** 4–10cm across, grey brown with a central umbo, often splitting radially at the edges. **Gills** whitish. **Stem** tough and whitish with long 'rooting' strands. Season late summer to autumn.

Melanoleuca melanoleuca *photographed 25 September*

Lyophyllum decastes *photographed 30 September*

Melanoleuca melaleuca is one of a group of mushrooms with broad flat caps and a central boss. Found on wood edges and woodland paths, one of its distinctive characteristics is the way the stem flesh discolours when cut. It is **edible** but not worthwhile. **Cap** 3–8cm across, dark brown with a central boss. **Gills** whitish and crowded. **Stem** whitish and covered with lateral brown fibres. When cut, the flesh of the stem is ochreous, especially at the base. Season late summer to late autumn.

Lyophyllum decastes grows in enormous clumps on the ground in open woodland throughout Britain, especially along pathsides. It is **edible** and fairly common. **Cap** 4–10cm across, grey-brown. **Gills** whitish or greyish. **Stem** white, sometimes brownish at the base when in large clumps. Season summer to autumn.

37

Clouded Agaric photographed 30 October

Club Foot photographed 19 October

Clouded Agaric

Clitocybe nebularis is common throughout Britain in deciduous or conifer woods and is often found in large rings or lines. It has a strong, sweetish smell. This mushroom is said to be **edible but it may cause stomach upsets. Cap** 5–20cm across, cloudy-grey, usually darker in the centre. **Gills** crowded, creamy, attached decurrently to the stem. **Stem** brittle and fibrous, usually swollen at the base. Season autumn to early winter.

Club Foot, *Clitocybe clavipes*, is also found in conifers and deciduous woods but is smaller than Clouded Agaric. It also has a much larger bulbous stem base. It has a strong smell and tastes of bitter almonds. It is **not edible. Cap** 4–8cm across, creamy or greyish coloured. **Gills** creamy-yellow attached down the stem (decurrent). **Stem** creamy with silky fibres, often very swollen at the base. Season autumn to early winter.

Clitocybe dealbata *photographed 17 October*

Common Funnel Cap photographed 28 September

Common Funnel Cap

Clitocybe infundibuliformis is found in deciduous woodlands or heaths, often on paths or road verges. **Cap** 3–8cm across, deeply depressed in the centre, pale pinkish-buff. **Gills** attached a long way down the stem (decurrent). **Stem** long, thicker at the base. Season summer to late autumn. **Edible**, but poor.

Tawny Funnel Cap, *Clitocybe flaccida*, is similar but much more orangy coloured, and is found in coniferous woods. **Edible**, but poor. *Clitocybe dealbata* is found growing in rings in pastures or lawns. It smells and tastes mealy and is **deadly poisonous**. Make sure not to confuse it with the Field Mushroom whose pink or blackish gills are the most obvious distinguishing characteristic. **Cap** 2–5cm across, white, usually with a greyish shine. **Gills** white. **Stem** white. Season summer to late autumn. Very similar and also **deadly poisonous** is *Clitocybe rivulosa*. It, too, is small and white but it lacks the greyish tints on the cap.

Amethyst Deceiver photographed 9 October

The Deceiver photographed 21 September

The Deceiver

Laccaria laccata is one of the most common mushrooms in Britain and is found in woods and on heaths. The colour, shape and size varies a great deal which is why it is known as 'the deceiver'. **Edible** but not worthwhile. **Cap** 2–6cm across, brick-red to pale cream in colour, the edges often wrinkled. **Gills** pinky. **Stem** tough and fibrous, pinkish, often twisted. Season summer to early winter.

Amethyst Deceiver, *Laccaria amethystea*, is one of the first common mushrooms that people learn to recognise, because of its lovely violet colours. It is found in all types of woods throughout Britain, but most commonly with beech. It is **edible** and quite good. **Cap** 1–5cm across, deep purple when wet, drying very pale lilac or creamy. **Gills** purplish. **Stem** fibrous, purplish, with a lovely lilac down at the base (tomentum). Season late summer to early winter.

Wood Woolly-foot photographed 27 August

Collybia dryophila *photographed 9 September*

Wood Woolly-foot

Collybia peronata is very common and can be found in both deciduous and conifer woods throughout Britain. The base of the stem is hairy and leaf litter is always attached to it. **Not edible** due to its acrid taste. **Cap** 2–6cm across, light tan to brown, leathery and wrinkled with age. **Gills** yellowish or tan. **Stem** thin with lots of shortish hairs at the base. Season late summer to late autumn.

Collybia dryophila is found in clumps in deciduous woods and is also very common. Although it is **edible** it is really too small and tough to eat. **Cap** 2–5cm across, flattened and often wavy at maturity, usually whitish-buff but may be darker. **Gills** creamish coloured. **Stem** swollen at the base which usually has leaves attached to it. Season early summer to late autumn.

45

Spotted Tough-shank photographed 3 October

Spindle Shank photographed 12 October

Spotted Tough-shank

Collybia maculata is one of the most common woodland mushrooms and is found in both deciduous and conifer woods. **Not edible** due to its bitter flavour and tough texture. **Cap** 5–10cm across, at first white then usually spotted or marked with rust-coloured stains. **Gills** very crowded, white or pale cream, also gradually becoming rusty coloured. **Stem** is normally long, white then spotted rusty, rooting. Season summer to late autumn.

Spindle Shank, *Collybia fusipes*, grows in large clumps at the base of oak and, occasionally, beech trees. The Latin name *fusipes* means fused feet and derives from the fact that the stems fuse together at the base until they seem to spring from a common stem. **Not edible. Cap** 3–7cm across, red-brown, darker when wet. **Gills** cream. **Stem** cream, getting very dark at base. Season summer to late autumn.

Butter Cap photographed 1 November

The Goblet photographed 19 October

Butter Cap

Collybia butyracea is very common late in the season in both deciduous and conifer woods. It has a distinctly greasy texture to the cap which gives it its common name. **Edible** but not worthwhile. **Cap** 3–7cm across, dark brown to light tan with a central boss (umbo). **Gills** whitish, crowded. **Stem** same colour as cap, swollen at base. Season autumn to early winter.

The Goblet, *Cantharellula cyathiformis*, has a very dark brown, distinctly funnel-shaped cap. It is found in leaf litter or on rotten logs in mixed woods. **Edible** but hardly worthwhile. **Cap** 2–7cm across, dark brown, funnel-shaped with an inrolled rim. **Gills** grey, running slightly down the stem (decurrent). **Stem** grey with a silky covering, swollen and downy at the base. Season late autumn to winter.

Goat Moth Wax Cap photographed 1 October

Velvet Shank photographed 10 December

Goat Moth Wax Cap

Hygrophorus cossus is quite common in mixed woodland, especially beech woods on chalk. **Not edible** partly due to its strong taste and smell which resembles the Goat Moth Larva. **Cap** 3–7cm across, white, sometimes buff near the centre, slimy to the touch. **Gills** whitish, slightly attached down the stem (decurrent). **Stem** whitish, slimy. Season autumn.

Velvet Shank, *Flammulina velutipes*, grows, often in clumps, on decaying trees, especially elms. It is **edible**. **Cap** 2–9cm across, yellowish-orange. **Gills** pale yellowish, crowded. **Stem** yellowish at the top blackish-brown below, covered in dense velvety hairs, hence its common name. Season early to mid winter.

Hygrocybe langei *photographed 9 September*

Conical Wax Cap photographed 2 October

Blackening Wax Cap

Hygrocybe nigrescens is quite common in grassland. It blackens when bruised, or with age, until it looks as if it is made of charcoal. **Edible. Cap** 3–6cm across, bluntly conical, orange or scarlet, blackening. **Gills** pale yellow, blackening. **Stem** yellow or scarlet with white base, blackening. Season summer to late autumn.

Very similar is **Conical Wax Cap**, *Hygrocybe conica*, which is yellower in colour and has a more sharply conical cap. It also blackens, in all parts. **Edible**, but not recommended. *Hygrocybe langei* is a beautiful, yellow, conical mushroom that is found in grassland. **Edible. Cap** 2–7cm across, lemon-yellow to orange, often sharply conical, sticky to the touch. **Gills** yellow. **Stem** yellow. Season summer to late autumn. Very similar is *Hygrocybe konradii*, which is also found in grassland. Its distinguishing feature is that the yellow stem is white at the base.

False Chanterelle

False Chanterelle photographed 17 September

False Chanterelle

Hygrophoropsis aurantiaca is found in conifer woods and on heaths throughout Britain, often in large numbers. It is the mushroom most likely to be confused with the real Chanterelle (p. 135) but probably with no real harm done as it is known to be **edible**; a friend of mine, however, did have alarming hallucinations, apparently from eating this mushroom. It is distinguished from the Chanterelle by being more orange in colour, much tougher and more fibrous in texture, and generally smaller.

Cap 2–8cm across, shallowly funnel-shaped, orangy-yellow. **Gills** yellowish or orange, attached down the stem (decurrent), and often forked. **Stem** same colour as cap or darker. Season autumn.

Fairy Ring Champignon

Fairy Ring Champignon photographed 9 August

Fairy Ring Champignon

Marasmius oreades is one of the most common grassland species growing, as the English name implies, in rings and found throughout Britain. They are one of the most well-known **edible** mushrooms although the flavour is rather slight. They can be dried for storage extremely easily and in fact may often be half dry when you find them. Only the caps are eaten. Take care that you do not confuse this mushroom with *Clitocybe dealbata* or *C. rivulosa* (p. 41).

Cap 2–5cm across, creamy-buff coloured with a large central boss (umbo). **Gills** cream. **Stem** tough and rigid, whitish. Season late spring to late autumn.

Mycena pura *photographed 14 October*

Mycena galericulata *photographed 3 October*

Bonnet Mycena

Mycena galericulata grows in clusters on stumps and fallen, broadleaved trees. **Edible** but not worthwhile. **Cap** 2–6cm across, conical or bell shaped, brown or grey-brown with a lined margin. **Gills** white at first becoming flesh-pink later. **Stem** long, thin, tough, often rooting at the base which is covered in small hairs. Season all year except the coldest months.

Mycena pura is fairly common in beech woods and is distinguished by its shade of pale lilac or pink and by a strong smell like radish. **Edible. Cap** 2–6cm across, greyish-lilac or purplish or pinkish, lined at margin. **Gills** whitish-pink. **Stem** pinkish. Base covered in fine hairs. Season summer to winter.

Fleecy Milk-cap photographed 18 October

Peppery Milk-cap photographed 10 September

Fleecy Milk-cap

Lactarius vellereus is a very large, white mushroom with a cap surface that feels like wash-leather. Found in deciduous woods, most commonly in association with birch trees, it releases copious quantities of white milk when damaged. **Edible**, but very hot. **Cap** 10–25cm across, eventually with a depressed centre, white or creamish often staining yellow. The surface has a short woolly texture. Milk white. **Gills** brittle, pale cream. **Stem** short, thick and velvety. Season late summer to late autumn.

Peppery Milk-cap, *Lactarius piperatus*, is a very hot-tasting, white mushroom that is also found in deciduous woods but is smaller than Fleecy Milk-cap and with a much longer stem. **Edible** only in small amounts to add a peppery taste to other mushrooms. **Cap** 6–15cm across, creamy white, funnel-shaped. **Gills** very crowded, white or creamy. Milk white. **Stem** white. Season late summer to autumn.

Lactarius chrysorheus *photographed 5 October*

Grey Milk-cap photographed 5 October

Grey Milk-cap

Lactarius vietus is rather common under birch trees throughout Britain. The taste is acrid and hot. **Not edible. Cap** 3–8cm across, greyish-violet or pale brownish, slimy when moist. When damaged it exudes a white milk which turns grey or greenish gradually. **Gills** crowded, whitish-buff. **Stem** greyish, fragile, especially near the base. Season autumn.

Lactarius chrysorheus is a small, biscuity-coloured mushroom found in deciduous woods mainly with beech or oak. The milk is white at first but then quickly turns yellow. **Not edible. Cap** 3–8cm across, pinky-buff coloured, the centre becomes depressed when mature, usually with concentric bands of darker colour. When damaged it exudes a white milk which in a few seconds turns yellow. The taste is slightly bitter then gradually hot. **Gills** creamy-buff. **Stem** creamy-buff. Season late summer to autumn.

Saffron Milk-cap photographed 6 September

Woolly Milk-cap photographed 6 October

Saffron Milk-cap

Lactarius deliciosus is found under conifers, as is *Lactarius deterrimus*. Both exude an orange milk but in *L. deterrimus* the milk goes purplish in ten minutes and wine-red in half an hour, while *L. deliciosus* just goes a dull orange. Both are **edible. Cap** 3–10cm across, background creamy-buff with concentric bands of orangy-red, rather brittle. **Gills** apricot colour then staining green with age or after bruising. **Stem** creamy, often with orange spots, becoming greenish. Season late summer to autumn.

Woolly Milk-cap, *Lactarius torminosus*, is **poisonous** and found in association with birch trees. **Cap** 4–12cm across, pinky-salmon colour with darker concentric bands. Margin inrolled and covered with dense woolly hairs. All parts exude a white milk which is hot and acrid to taste. **Gills** flesh coloured. **Stem** creamy coloured. Season late summer to autumn.

65

Ugly Milk-cap photographed 10 October

Slimy Milk-cap photographed 27 September

Ugly Milk-cap

Lactarius turpis is such a dull colour that you can easily miss it in the grass under birches, where it is found. It is extremely hot to the taste. **Not edible. Cap** 5–20cm across, dirty olive-green with darker concentric bands. All parts exude a white milk when damaged. **Gills** creamy-buff, crowded. **Stem** greenish-olive, short and stout, often pitted. Season late summer to late autumn.

Slimy Milk-cap, *Lactarius blennius*, is found in deciduous woods, most commonly under beech. **Edible**, it can be eaten in moderation if well cooked. **Cap** olive-grey or pale brownish with darker blotches in concentric bands. Slimy when wet. All parts exude a white milk when damaged. The taste is very hot and acrid. **Gills** creamy, bruising greyish. **Stem** pale grey or pale olive. Season late summer to late autumn.

Lactarius pyrogalus *photographed 22 September*

Rufous Milk-cap photographed 12 October

Rufous Milk-cap

Lactarius rufus is commonly found in pine woods. It is **edible**, but is so hot to taste that it will really 'burn' your tongue after about one minute, although a single mushroom can be added to a dish in place of pepper. **Cap** 3–9cm across, red brown, centrally depressed with a central umbo. All parts exude a white milk when damaged. **Gills** creamy. **Stem** same colour as cap. Season summer to late autumn.

Lactarius pyrogalus is only found under hazel bushes where it sometimes forms a complete ring around a bush. It is very hot tasting and is **best not eaten. Cap** 5–10cm across, creamy-buff or dingy grey usually with darker concentric bands, exudes a white milk when damaged. **Gills** creamy-ochre coloured. **Stem** similar but lighter in colour than the cap. Season autumn.

Lactarius subdulcis *photographed 2 October*

Oak Milk-cap photographed 27 September

Oak Milk-cap

Lactarius quietus is very common under oaks. It is **edible** and tastes mild or a touch bitter. **Cap** 3–8cm across, biscuity-brown, nearly always with distinct, darker concentric bands. Exudes whitish-cream milk. **Gills** browny cream. **Stem** same colour as cap. Season autumn.

Lactarius subdulcis is one of the most common milk-caps found in deciduous woods, especially beech. The white coloured milk and the lack of concentric bands on the cap help to determine this species. **Edible. Cap** 3–7cm across, buff-brown to rusty-brown. Milk plentiful, exudes from all parts when damaged. **Gills** creamy-buff, developing rusty patches as it ages. **Stem** the same colour as cap but lighter. Season late summer to late autumn.

Blackening Russula

Blackening Russula photographed 16 September

Blackening Russula

Russula nigricans is a very common mushroom found under both deciduous and conifer trees. It is a most distinctive *russula* starting out white, reddening when cut or broken, and eventually going completely black all over. It is **edible** but rather tasteless, with a slight hotness. **Cap** 5–20cm across, dirty white, becoming brown and eventually black. **Gills** cream, widely spaced, brittle, reddish or bruising, eventually blackening. **Stem** white or brown, finally black. Season summer to autumn.

Russula densifolia is similar to the Blackening Russula but has many more gills and neither reddens nor blackens as much. Season summer to autumn. **Edible**, but poor.

Fetid Russula

Fetid Russula photographed 26 August

Fetid Russula

Russula foetens is very common and is remarkable for its glutinous or slimy cap and strong, rancid, oily smell. It is found under both deciduous and conifer trees throughout Britain. **Not edible. Cap** 5–14cm across, honey coloured, darker in the centre, slimy. The margin is distinctly furrowed. **Gills** creamy, often with brown spots. **Stem** honey coloured. Season late summer to late autumn.

Russula laurocerasi is similar to the Fetid Russula but has a strong smell of bitter almonds and usually is also a little smaller. It is found under both deciduous and conifer trees. **Not edible.**

The Sickener photographed 8 October

Beechwood Sickener photographed 29 September

The Sickener

Russula emetica is common in pine woods and is a most attractive, bright red mushroom with an extremely hot, bitter taste like bile. **Poisonous.** Cap 3–9cm across, bright cherry red. **Gills** pure white to creamy. **Stem** long, pure white, fragile. You have to be very gentle to collect a complete one. The stem is often swollen especially towards the base. Season summer to late autumn.

Beechwood Sickener, *Russula mairei*, is similar to The Sickener but grows under beeches, has a shorter stem and is more often washed out in colour and more frequently nibbled by slugs. It tastes hot and is **poisonous.** Cap 3–9cm across, red-pink or washed out to almost white. **Gills** white or creamish. **Stem** shortish, white. Season late summer to autumn.

Russula aeruginea *photographed 2 October*

Green Cracked Russula photographed 4 September

Green Cracked Russula

Russula virescens has a cap surface that cracks to show white below, leaving scaly patches of greenish surface. It is found in deciduous woods, especially under beech. A good **edible** species but unfortunately not very common. **Cap** 5–12cm across, green or washed out to pale green or even cream, often marking buff-orange where damaged. **Gills** creamy, brittle. **Stem** short, firm, discolouring buff-orange in places. Season summer to autumn.

Russula aeruginea is rather common under birch and is **edible**. **Cap** 4–10cm across, grassy-green or lighter, often with yellowish or brownish tints. The surface does not crack. **Gills** creamy coloured, forking. **Stem** white, fairly firm. Season summer to early autumn.

Russula xerampelina photographed *19 September*

The Charcoal Burner photographed 18 October

Russula xerampelina is a very variable mushroom and indeed some authorities have divided it into a number of species. The most distinctive field characteristic is the smell of crab you get from the gills, especially when they are crushed. A useful test is to rub the stem with iron salts which give a dull green reaction (most *russulas* give a pink reaction). **Edible** and fairly common under beech or oak. **Cap** 5–12cm across, dull brown to wine-red in colour. Firm. **Gills** cream to ochre coloured. **Stem** white, often with rosy tints, brownish or bruising. Season late summer to late autumn.

The Charcoal Burner, *Russula cyanoxantha*, is common and **very good to eat**. Found under broadleaved trees. **Cap** 5–15cm across, dull violet or purple or often greenish or a mixture of the two. Firm. **Gills** white, oily and flexible to the touch. **Stem** white, giving only a very slight greenish-grey tint with iron salts. Season summer to late autumn.

Common Yellow Russula photographed 25 October

Geranium-scented Russula photographed 11 October

Geranium-scented Russula

Russula fellea is common under beeches. Its outstanding characteristic is that all parts are straw coloured and have a distinctive scent of geranium. If you cup the mushrooms in your hand before smelling them it will be more noticeable. The taste is very hot. **Not edible. Cap** 4–9cm across, straw or honey coloured, slightly sticky when moist. **Gills** straw coloured. **Stem** straw coloured, lighter than cap. Season late summer to late autumn.

Common Yellow Russula, *Russula ochroleuca*, is very common, often until quite late in the season, under deciduous and conifer trees. **Edible** but not good as the taste is usually hot. **Cap** 4–10cm across, ochre to greenish-yellow. **Gills** creamy coloured. **Stem** white, greying slightly with age. Season autumn to late autumn.

Russula sardonia *photographed 5 October*

Yellow Swamp Russula photographed 7 September

Yellow Swamp Russula

Russula claroflava is a most beautiful, bright yellow colour and is fairly common under birches, especially in wet areas. **Edible** and very nice. **Cap** 4–10cm across, bright yellow. **Gills** a strong creamy-yellow. **Stem** white, greying with age. Season occasionally in summer, normally autumn.

Russula sardonia is common under pines and the lovely grey-violet tints on the stem are a distinctive feature. Taste very hot. **Not edible. Cap** 4–10cm across, purplish-brown to violet or washed out by rain to almost white. **Gills** primrose-yellow to ochre-yellow. **Stem** grey-violet or purplish, occasionally pure white. Season summer to autumn.

Blackish-purple Russula photographed 18 September

Russula caerulia *photographed 11 October*

Blackish-purple Russula

Russula atropurpurea is one of the most common *russulas* especially under oak or beech. Taste hot. **Edible, but only when cooked. Cap** 4–10cm across, often almost black. When young it has the appearance of a conker, but later expands to purply-red with a darker centre and eventually becomes pinky-reddish, with mottled brownish spots. **Gills** pale cream. **Stem** white, greying with age. Season late summer to late autumn.

Russula caerulea is a remarkably perfect-looking *russula* – dark purple with a definite umbo – which is quite common under pine, especially in Scotland. **Edible**, with a mild taste. **Cap** 3–8cm across, purple or livid violet with a pointed umbo. **Gills** pale ochre colour. **Stem** white, thicker in the middle. Season late summer to autumn.

Rose-gilled Grisette

Rose-gilled Grisette photographed 12 August

Rose-gilled Grisette

Volvariella speciosa has a sac-like volva like an *amanita*. The main difference is that the gills will be pink on maturity due to the pink spore print but the young gills are white like an *amanita*. It is **edible** but you should never eat it unless you are certain of your identification because of the possibility of confusing it with a poisonous *amanita*. Found sometimes in large quantities on manured fields, manure heaps or on rotting straw.

Cap 5–10cm across, whitish or grey, centre darker more browny, viscid when moist. **Gills** white then pink then pinky-brown. **Stem** white, tapering upwards from the basal bulb which is contained in a greyish, sac-like volva. Season summer to late autumn.

Wood Blewit

Wood Blewit photographed 7 November

Wood Blewit

Lepista nuda is a mushroom which, in a good year, can be found by the bucketful in almost any kind of woodland, hedgerow or garden. It grows from a dense white mat of cottony fibres (mycelium) which can be seen developing in deep leaf litter before the mushrooms come. November is usually the best month to find these strongly-scented mushrooms. They are **edible** and good, but only when cooked.

Cap 6–12cm across, purply-lilac colour at first then becoming a sort of milk-chocolate brown. **Gills** strongly purple at first fading to creamy-buff with age. **Stem** purplish, of a fibrous texture, and swollen at the base. Season late autumn to early winter.

Field Blewit or Blue-leg photographed 26 October

Lepista irina *photographed 8 October*

Field Blewit or Blue-leg

Lepista saeva is an excellent **edible** mushroom, found in old grassland, often growing in rings. Unlike Wood Blewits on the previous page it lacks the purple gills but it does have a purplish-blue colour on the stem, hence the common name Blue-leg. It has a strong, perfumed smell. **Cap** 6–10cm across, creamy to brownish. **Gills** white to flesh coloured. **Stem** creamy coloured with distinct bluish-violet markings. Short, swollen at the base, often two or more join at the base. Season autumn to early winter.

Lepista irina is a good **edible** mushroom but unfortunately not common. It grows in woods and has a strong, perfumed smell that some find garlicky. **Cap** 5–11cm across, creamy-brown. **Gills** flesh coloured becoming light brown. **Stem** dirty white with a fibrous cover, often twisted. Season autumn.

The Miller

The Miller photographed 15 October

The Miller

Clitopilus prunulus is very common in grassy woodlands and is **good to eat**, especially when young. The smell is strongly mealy and the gills take on a pink tinge as they mature. However, be extremely certain before eating Millers as there are at least three poisonous species which resemble them: *Clitocybe dealbata* and *Clitocybe rivulosa* (p. 41) and *Entoloma sinuatum* (below). **Cap** 3–10cm across, generally smallish, often wavy at the edge, white or greyish. **Gills** white then pale, creamy-pink, decurrent. **Stem** thin. Season summer to late autumn.

Enteloma sinuatum is found in deciduous woods and wood edges but is fairly rare. It has a mealy smell and is **deadly poisonous**. **Cap** 6–20cm, ivory or dull grey-brown. **Gills** creamy then pinkish, flesh coloured. **Stem** white. Season late summer to late autumn.

Pluteus salicimus *photographed 13 September*

Common Fawn Pluteus photographed 6 September

Common Fawn Pluteus

Pluteus cervinus is common throughout Britain on rotten wood and dead stumps of deciduous trees and occasionally conifers. Large specimens can also be found on sawdust heaps. **Edible** but not worthwhile. **Cap** 4–12cm across, light to dark brown with radiating streaks, often wrinkled. **Gills** start out white and then go dull pink, crowded. **Stem** streaked with brown fibres, sometimes swollen at the base. Season any time of year.

Pluteus salicinus is found on rotting deciduous wood, especially willow. **Edible** but not worthwhile. **Cap** 2–6cm across, a lovely grey with slight greenish tints and a darker umbo. **Gills** white at first then pink. **Stem** tall, usually pure white, sometimes tinged grey at the base. Season spring to late autumn.

Cortinarius obtusus *photographed 15 October*

Cortinarius pseudosalor *photographed 1 October*

Cortinarius pseudosalor is one of the most common members of *Cortinarius*, the largest world-wide genus of larger mushrooms. *C. pseudosalor* has a sticky cap and stem which puts it into the *Myxacium* group. It can be found in both coniferous and deciduous woods, especially under beech. **Edibility unknown. Cap** 3–8cm across, pale ochre to deep brown, margin often paler, sticky when moist, drying shiny, often wrinkled. **Gills** pale cream then ochre and finally rusty. **Stem** white but usually with violet tints, sticky. Season autumn.

Cortinarius obtusus is one of the *Telamonia* group of *Cortinarius*. The whole mushroom has a radishy smell and is found in conifer woods. **Edibility unknown. Cap** 1–5cm across, red brown when wet, drying out to light tan. **Gills** ochre-cinnamon colour then more rusty coloured. **Stem** yellowish to white, tapering downwards. Season spring to late autumn.

Cortinarius trivialis *photographed 23 September*

Red-banded Cortinarius photographed 16 October

Red-banded Cortinarius

Cortinarius armillatus is the most well-known member of the genus, distinguished by its large size and the orange bands on the stem. It is found mainly with birch trees. **Edible**, but best avoided as there are similar poisonous ones. **Cap** 4–12cm across, rusty-brown when mature, paler when young. **Gills** milk-coffee colour at first then rusty-brown. **Stem** tall, nearly always with one or two orangy bands of veil remnants, base usually swollen. Season autumn.

Cortinarius trivialis is quite common in wet woods usually with alder or willow. **Edibility unknown. Cap** 3–9cm across, light ochreous to dark ochreous brown in colour, very sticky when moist, shiny when dry. The edge is often wrinkled. **Gills** pale buff then more rusty as spores develop. **Stem** similar colour to cap, covered in whitish, flakey scales, very sticky. Season autumn.

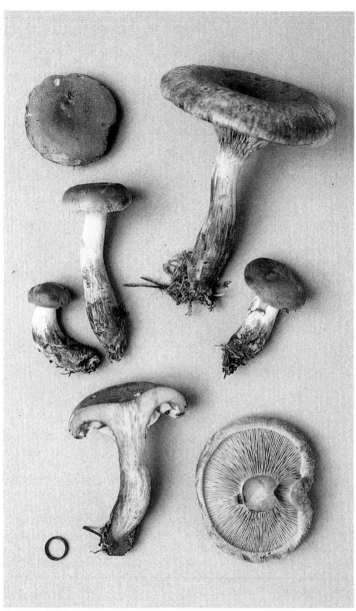

Brown Roll Rim

Brown Roll Rim photographed 19 September

Brown Roll Rim

Paxillus involutus is extremely common in broadleaved woods and acid heathland, especially with birch. It is rather variable in appearance but once you get your eye in you will be able to distinguish it with ease. The main features are that the cap is an olive-ochre colour, and rolled under at the edge. **Deadly poisonous**. Some books recommend eating this mushroom but it has now been proved to contain poisons which accumulate over repeated doses and will eventually kill.

Cap 5–12cm across, ochreous with an olivaceous tint becoming rusty-brown with age, sticky when wet, woolly especially at the rim. **Gills** run down the stem (decurrent), ochre coloured, bruising reddish. **Stem** pale ochre, bruising reddish. Season late summer to late autumn.

Gymnopilus junonius *photographed 29 September*

Shaggy Pholiota photographed 27 September

Gymnopilus junonius is a very striking mushroom which grows on the stumps, logs or buried wood of deciduous trees in large clumps. Taste bitter. **Not edible. Cap** 5–15cm across, rich golden-yellow, covered in small scales. **Gills** yellow then rusty-brown. **Stem** with a distinct ring, swollen lower down, then diminishing to a narrow point. Season late summer to early winter.

Shaggy Pholiota, *Pholiota squarrosa*, grows in large clumps at the base of deciduous trees and occasionally conifers. **Best not eaten** but young ones can be eaten if boiled and the water discarded before cooking, although do not drink alcohol with them as they can cause palpitations and vomiting. **Cap** 3–10cm across, ochre coloured, densely covered with upright scales. **Gills** pale yellowy-cream, later darker. **Stems** very scaly with ring near the top, narrow at the base. Season autumn.

Hebeloma crustuliniforme *photographed 21 October*

Hebeloma sinapizans *photographed 13 October*

Poison Pie

Hebeloma crustuliniforme has a bitter taste and a strong radishy smell. It is found in open mixed woodland and wood edges and is **poisonous**, causing vomiting and diarrhoea. **Cap** 4–10cm across, pale ochre-tan coloured, greasy when moist. **Gills** creamy then milky-coffee coloured. They exude water droplets when moist. **Stem** whitish, incrusted with mealy spots, especially at the top. Season late summer to late autumn.

Hebeloma sinapizans is the biggest and stoutest of the *Hebelomas*. **Poisonous**. **Cap** 4–12 or even 20cm across, convex then flattened, ochre, brownish, paling to cream at the margin. **Gills** pale buff colour. **Stem** rather thick with a swollen base. Season autumn.

Inocybe geophylla *var.* lilacina *photographed* 7 *October*

Red-staining Inocybe photographed 16 July

Red-staining Inocybe

Inocybe patouillardii is **deadly poisonous** but all *inocybes* should be avoided as they are dangerous to eat. Found on chalky soils, often early in the season, it is best distinguished by the way it reddens when damaged. **Cap** 2–7cm across, ivory coloured, staining red or rusty. The cap has a fibrous silky appearance. **Gills** creamy-pink at first then pale olive-brown. **Stem** creamy, often with a small bulb. Season spring to autumn.

Inocybe geophylla, small, pure white or lilac to purple in the variety *lilacina*, both are found in either deciduous or conifer woods, often on pathsides or ditch edges. **Poisonous**. **Cap** 1.5–3.5cm across, conical, fibrous, silky-white or lilac. **Gills** pale cream at first, eventually pale brownish from the spores. **Stem** narrow, silky and fibrous, pure white or violet. Season summer to autumn.

Yellow Cow-pat Toadstool photographed 17 August

Panaeolus semiovatus *photographed 19 October*

Yellow Cow-pat Toadstool

Bolbitius vitellinus is a most attractive little yellow mushroom that is found on manure, rotten straw or wood chips. **Not edible. Cap** 1–4cm across, chrome-yellow at first fading to pale greyish-brown as it ages. **Gills** pale yellow then brown. **Stem** long and thin, delicate, pale whitish-yellow at first then buff. Season summer to late autumn.

Panaeolus semiovatus common on dung, at almost any time of year after rain. **Not edible. Cap** 2–6cm across, bell-shaped, clay white, sticky when wet, drying shiny. **Gills** broad, dark brown with a white edge. **Stem** tall and narrow with a delicate white ring.

Sulphur Tuft, note the dark spores on the cap surface

Sulphur Tuft photographed 14 September

Sulphur Tuft

Hypholoma fasciculare is definitely our most commonly recorded mushroom; what a pity it is **not edible**. It is found growing in very large clusters on stumps of deciduous or conifer trees, and sometimes on old wooden fencing. It tastes very bitter. **Cap** 2–6cm across, orangy in the middle, yellow towards the edge, frequently with greenish (sulphurous) tints. The rim is often hung with a yellow veil. **Gills** pale sulphur-yellow, then darkening eventually to dark brown. **Stem** sulphur-yellow, but usually brownish at the base, often showing a faint ring zone. Season spring to late winter.

Galerina mutabilis grows in similar large clumps on deciduous trees but is **edible** and tastes mild and good. It is a little larger, orangy-buff in colour, drying creamy from the centre out. The stem has brownish scales and a distinct ring zone.

Horse Mushroom

Horse Mushroom photographed 11 October

Horse Mushroom

Agaricus arvensis is an excellent **edible** species which, in a good year, can be found in great quantities. It grows in old grassland or wood edges, often in rings which can fruit year after year, sometimes for hundreds of years. Take care not to confuse it with the poisonous Yellow Stainer (p. 116) which is rather similar. Whilst both mushrooms yellow when touched, the Yellow Stainer is dinstinctly yellow in the stem base when a fresh one is cut. The Horse Mushroom is larger than the Yellow Stainer and has a distinct smell of aniseed, especially when cut.

Cap 8–20cm across, creamy-white, yellowing slightly on bruising or with age. **Gills** white in young buttons, then pink and finally dark brown. *Stem* white with a large double ring, bruising yellowish. Season late summer to autumn.

Yellow Stainer

Yellow Stainer photographed 24 October

Yellow Stainer

Agaricus xanthodermus is related to field and shop mushrooms but it is **poisonous**, causing sweating, flushing and very severe stomach cramps in some people. Yellow Stainers are found most typically in hedges but also in woods, wood edges, fields and gardens. Tastes unpleasant and smells inky.

Cap 5–15cm across, rounded at first then flattening. White in colour, when fresh it bruises yellow very rapidly. **Gills** white at first then pale pink, finally brown. **Stem** normally long, often curved with a large ring, yellowing when touched. The base of the stem is yellow inside when cut. Season summer to autumn.

Field Mushroom

Field Mushroom photographed 23 October

Field Mushroom

Agaricus campestris is the most commonly eaten wild mushroom in Britain but it is fast disappearing along with its natural habitat of old grassland and pastures, as these are being ploughed for arable crops. **Lovely to eat** raw or cooked but take care not to confuse it with the poisonous Yellow Stainer (p. 116) which bruises yellow, while Field Mushrooms bruise pinkish. Another danger is the poisonous *Clitocybes* (p. 41) which have white gills and smell of meal.

Cap 3–10cm across, white then creamy coloured, staying a long time in the button stage. Taste and smell of mushrooms. The flesh tends to go pinkish when cut. **Gills** pink even when the buttons are tiny, then reddish, finally dark brown. **Stem** whitish. The ring remains attached to the cap for a long time. Season late summer to late autumn.

Agaricus langei

Agaricus silvaticus *photographed 25 September*

Agaricus silvaticus is found in coniferous woods and is one of the mushroom genus which goes bright blood-red on cutting. It **makes excellent eating.** **Cap** 5–10cm across, covered in brown fibres which group together to form scales. The flesh reddens on cutting. **Gills** pale at first then pinkish, finally brown. **Stem** bulbous, whitish, sometimes with brownish scales below the brownish ring. Season summer to autumn.

Agaricus langei is very similar to *Agaricus silvaticus* but grows in mixed woods and the stem is not bulbous. The cap's scale colour also seems to be more orangy. **Excellent to eat.**

Agaricus haemorrhoidarius is a very similar to the two above but grows specifically in deciduous woods. The stem does have a basal bulb. **Excellent to eat.**

Psathyrella hydrophila *photographed 30 September*

Liberty Cap photographed 1 October

Psathyrella hydrophila is found in dense tufts in damp areas of deciduous woodland. **Edible** but not worthwhile. **Cap** 2–3cm across, semi-globular, brown, paler in the centre as it drys. The edge is covered with white, woolly, veil remnants, especially when young. **Gills** creamy, then chocolate-brown. **Stem** long, fragile, white-brownish below. Season late spring to late autumn. *Psathyrella candolleana* is larger than *P. hydrophila* and pale ochreous or whitish in colour. It grows in tufts on old wood, especially cut stumps. **Edibility unknown.**

Liberty Cap, *Psilocybe semilanceata*, is quite common in grassland and has a bonnet-shaped cap with a tiny umbo in the middle, resembling the caps worn at the time of the French Revolution, hence its common name. It is hallucinogenic. **Cap** 0.5–1.5cm across, cream coloured with a darker edge. **Gills** cream, then purplish-brown. **Stems** very long and thin, white or cream. Season late summer to late autumn.

Weeping Widow

Weeping Widow photographed 29 September

Weeping Widow

Lacrymaria velutina commonly grows in grassy areas of woods, paths and roadsides throughout Britain. It is seen to 'weep' when the gills form droplets of water when moist, hence its common name. It is **edible** but has a bitter flavour.

Cap 2–10cm across, ochre in colour with an orange centre. The whole cap is covered in woolly fibrils which hang down in small tufts over the cap edge. **Gills** brown with a white edge then blackish, mottled, 'weeping'. **Stem** long, often joined together at the base in groups of 2–20, but not always. Whitish at the top more ochre-red towards the base, covered in woolly fibrils below the ring zone. Season summer to late autumn.

Shaggy Ink Cap or Lawyer's Wig

Shaggy Ink Cap or Lawyer's Wig photographed 26 August

Shaggy Ink Cap or Lawyer's Wig

Coprinus comatus is very common in grass, by roadsides, in lawns or rubbish heaps, especially where the soil has been recently disturbed. This is an excellent **edible** species but it does not keep more than an hour or two. Only the white buttons are good to eat and once the gills start to blacken it must be discarded.

Cap 5–15cm across, sausage shaped when a button, then conical, quickly disintegrating. White and shaggy, light brown in the centre breaking up into scales. **Gills** start out white then pinken from the base and then rapidly blacken and start to rot (deliquesce). In fact they autodigest from the bottom upwards to free a new area of gill to drop spores. **Stem** very tall, white, with a swollen rotting base and loose ring. Season summer to late autumn.

Glistening Ink Cap photographed 17 June

Common Ink Cap photographed 11 October

Common Ink Cap

Coprinus atramentarius is the mushroom that gives the genus its name, as ink used to be made by boiling the blackened (deliquesced) caps in a little water and cloves. It grows in clumps on the soil but is associated with rotten wood. **Edible**, but must not be eaten in conjunction with alcohol as it causes nausea and palpitations. **Cap** 3–7cm across, oval, staying oval like the buttons for a long time. Whitish, greyish or fawnish, with scales near the centre. **Gills** white then gradually blackening. **Stem** white with base cut away like a sharpened pencil. Season spring to late autumn.

Glistening Ink Cap, *Coprinus micaceus*, is found in large clumps on stumps or buried wood. **Edible**. **Cap** 1–4cm across, cream to reddish in the centre then blackening. Covered in fine powdery (micaceus) particles. **Gills** white then brown, finally black. **Stem** white, fragile. Season late spring to late autumn.

Oyster Mushroom

Oyster Mushroom photographed 10 September

Oyster Mushroom

Pleurotus ostreatus is one of the most important **edible** mushrooms which is now sometimes grown commercially and thus available in the shops. It is found growing throughout Britain on standing trunks, stumps or fallen logs of deciduous trees, especially beech.

Cap 6–14cm across. The caps form in overlapping layers like tiles and are very variable in colour, ranging from white to cream, to brown or bluey-grey. The latter colour, being reminiscent of oysters, gives them their common name. **Gills** white, yellowing a little with age, attached down the stem (decurrent). **Stem** grows out of one side of the cap (excentric), and is often very short or absent. Season any time of the year, except when it is very cold, but mainly in the late summer and autumn.

Chroomgomphus rutilus *photographed 28 September*

Comphideus glutinosus *photographed 22 October*

Chroomgomphus rutilus is quite common in coniferous woods throughout Britain, especially pine. It tastes and smells a bit astringent. **Edible** but not worthwhile. **Cap** 4–14cm across, greasy but not really sticky, reddish-brown or reddish-fawn in colour. **Gills** buff then dirty purple, joined decurrently to the stem. **Stem** tapers towards the base, reddish at the top with chrome-yellow colours at the base, slightly sticky. Season autumn.

Gomphideus glutinosus is found with conifers, especially spruce. **Edible** but not worthwhile. **Cap** 4–12cm across, very glutinous and sticky, greyish-violet to fawnish-brown in colour. **Gills** white then greyish, connected down the stem (decurrent). **Stem** white with a chrome-yellow base, very sticky below ring zone. Season autumn.

Gomphideus roseus is very similar but the cap is a lovely, pinky-red colour. **Edible** but not recommended.

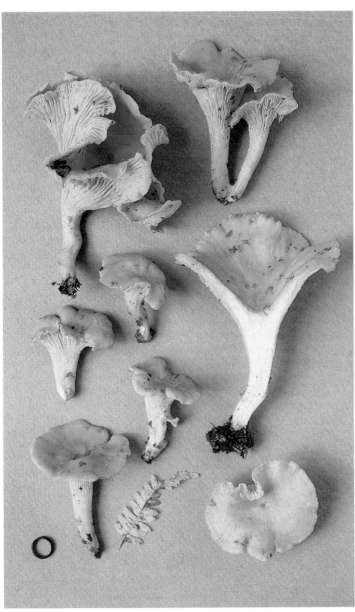

Chanterelle

Chanterelle photographed 1 September

Chanterelle

Cantharellus cibarius can be found in all kinds of woodlands but I find them most often in association with birch and pine. In some areas, especially in Scotland, they can be collected in large quantities. Chanterelles are one of the foremost **edible** species as they keep quite well and are excellent cooked with potatoes and bacon. They have a mild, fragrant smell, reminiscent of apricots.

Cap 3–11cm across, depressed in the centre and often wavy at the edge. Bright apricot-yellow or a little paler or darker. **Gills** are individually rather shallow, more like veins. They are attached decurrently to the stem and are yellow like the cap. **Stem** thick and stubby or fairly long, narrower at the base. Season summer to autumn.

Horn of Plenty or Black Trumpet

Horn of Plenty or Black Trumpet photographed 5 October

Horn of Plenty or Black Trumpets

Craterellus cornicupoides are found in deciduous woods, especially beech, but are difficult to spot amongst the dead leaves because of their dull blackish colour. However, once you have found one, grovel about among the leaves and you will probably be able to make a good collection as they are often found in clumps. To my way of thinking they are **one of the three top edibles**.

Cap 2–8cm across, black when wet, drying dark brownish. The cap is funnel-shaped and hollow right down into the stem, with the edge lobed and very wavy. **Gills** at most a few raised ridges in the lighter surface under the cap, ash-grey in colour. **Stem** a continuation of the surface under the cap, often darker at the base. Season late summer to late autumn.

Red-cracked Boletus

Red-cracked Boletus photographed 2 October

Red-cracked Boletus

Boletus chrysenteron is probably the most common boletus and is found throughout Britain under broadleaved trees, especially beech and oak. It is **edible** with a good flavour but goes mushy on cooking. I recommend drying the caps and then powdering them up to add to soups and stews for flavouring. **Cap** 4–11cm across, dingy olive-brown in colour, with a velvety texture cracking irregularly to show yellow and coral-pink flesh. **Pores and tubes** lemon-yellow, turning greenish with age. **Stem** yellow at the top normally with a pronounced area of red, brownish at the base. The cut flesh is yellowish turning a little blue above the gills and in the stem base. Season early to late autumn.

Boletus lanatus also cracks on the cap surface but lacks the coral-pink under the cap surface. The stem is normally marked with vertical ridges. **Edible**.

Cep

Cep photographed 10 October

Cep

Boletus edulis is the undoubted king of the **edible** mushrooms because of its excellent flavour, large weight and size, and the way it keeps its flavour when dried. I have been offered both the mother and grandmother of an Italian man I met for six good specimens I had in my basket! Young, fresh specimens are lovely to eat raw in salads, more mature specimens should be cooked. Found in all types of woodland throughout Britain.

Cap 8–20 or even 30cm across, brown or biscuity coloured, sometimes with a paler bloom, slightly greasy in wet weather. **Pores and tubes** white at first then becoming greyish and finally greenish. When they have discoloured the tubes should be removed and discarded before cooking. **Stem** creamy coloured with a fine white network (reticulum) of raised lines that are usually most noticeable near the top. Large and thick, often bulging and fat at the base. Season summer to late autumn.

Bay Boletus

Bay Boletus photographed 12 October

Bay Boletus

Boletus badius is another excellent **edible** *boletus*, and not usually as bug-infested as some ceps you will find. It grows in coniferous woods, also sometimes in deciduous woods, and is common. It is distinguished from other ceps by the way the pores bruise grey-blue and by its smaller size and the lack of network (reticulum) on the stem.

Cap 4–14cm across, chocolate-brown, sometimes a little reddish, smooth and polished when dry, a little sticky when wet. **Pores and tubes** whitish then pale greenish-yellow, quickly bruising blue-grey to the touch. The flesh when cut bruises slightly bluish. **Stem** is usually white at the top with brown markings below, normally not swollen or tapered. Season summer to late autumn.

Boletus luridus *photographed 12 July*

Boletus erythropus *photographed 8 October*

Boletus luridus is commonly found in wood edges in association with deciduous trees, especially oak and beech, on calcareous soils. **Cap** 6–14cm across, pale olive-brown with reddish areas, downy at first, bruising dark brown. The **tubes** are yellowish and the **pores** orange, both become strongly blue on bruising. **Stem** yellowish at the top, browny-reddish lower down with a network (reticulum) of fine reddish lines. Bruises strongly blue when cut except at the base which normally shows red. Season spring to late autumn. **Edible** only when cooked, but even so many cause gastric upsets.

Boletus erythropus is larger than *B. luridus* with a velvety brown cap, red pores and stem. Bruises bright blue, then indigo when cut.

Satan's Boletus, *Boletus satanus*, has a very large whitish cap and red or orange pores. Blues slightly when cut. Found on calcareous soils with beech or oak. **Poisonous.** For this reason I would avoid eating all red- or orange-pored boletus.

Brown Birch Boletus

Brown Birch Boletus photographed 27 September

Brown Birch Boletus

Leccinum scabrum is the most common of the tall stemmed boletus in the genus *Leccinum*. It is found only with birch trees. The caps are **edible** but not of high quality. **Cap** 5–15cm across, hazel or snuff-brown, tacky in wet weather, smooth when dry, usually soft when pressed. **Pores and tubes** white, then tending to a creamy colour. **Stem** long, narrower at the top, white and covered with brownish or blackish scales. Cut flesh does not change colour. Season summer to late autumn.

Leccinum holopus is white or pale cream in colour, found with birches and sphagnum moss. Cut flesh is slightly pinkish. **Edible**, but poor.

Leccinum carpini has an ochre or brown cap which cracks, found mainly with hornbeams (*Carpinus*). Cut flesh is strongly brown or black. **Edible**, but poor.

Leccinum quercinum *photographed 20 October*

Orange Birch Boletus photographed 12 September

Orange Birch Boletus

Leccinum versipelle is common under birches and **very good to eat**. It
blackens when cut up and cooked. **Cap** 8–20cm across, orange. The young
pores are grey but then go white and finally dirty yellowish, bruising
blue-grey, The tubes are white. **Stem** long, usually thicker at the base,
white with grey or brownish scales. The flesh when cut through goes
pinkish then blue-grey and finally blackish. Season summer to late
autumn.

Leccinum quercinum is found under oaks. The cap is brick-red and the
thick stem is covered with orange scales. Flesh turns pinky-grey when cut
but does not go nearly as dark as *L. versipelle* or *L. aurantiacum*. **Edible.**

Leccinum aurantiacum is found under aspens. The cap is brick-orange
and the tall stem is dotted with orange scales. The flesh goes pinky-grey
then gradually blackens. **Edible.**

Suillus bovinus

Suillus bovinus *photographed 30 September*

Suillus bovinus is very common in heathy conifer woods, especially with Scots pine. It is **edible** with a good flavour but it needs to have the slimy peel removed and then to be used only for flavouring as the texture is spongy. **Cap** 3–10cm across, orangy or pinky coloured, slimy. Both the tubes and pores are orange in colour and the latter are large and open often joining together in groups or lines. **Stem** the same colour as the cap, without a ring arising from a pinkish woolly area (mycelium). Season summer to autumn.

Suillus variagatus is fairly common with conifers. **Edible. Cap** 6–13cm across, ochre or a little olivaceous in colour, speckled with brown scales and rather dry in texture. **Pores and tubes** olivaceous-brown in colour, darker than the cap. **Stem** yellowish, lighter than the cap. Season late summer to autumn.

Suillus granulatus *photographed 21 June*

Slippery Jack photographed 13 October

Slippery Jack

Suillus luteus is common with conifers, especially Scots pine. **Edible**, but it is essential to first remove the slimy skin, then dry and use for flavouring, because of the spongy texture. **Cap** 5–12cm across, chestnut-brown covered in a thick lilacy-tinted gluten. **Pores and tubes** yellow; pores small. **Stem** has a large floppy ring, whitish-brown and slimy below, yellowish with granular dots above. Season autumn.

Suillus granulatus is common under conifers. **Edible after peeling** but used only for flavouring, due to its spongy texture. **Cap** 3–9cm across, orange or yellow, sticky or shiny when dry. **Pores and tubes** lemon-yellow, exuding milky droplets. **Stem** whitish or lemon-yellow, upper region covered in whitish granules, hence 'granulatus'. Exudes pale milky droplets especially near the pores. Season late spring, summer or autumn.

Larch Boletus

Larch Boletus photographed 22 September

Larch Boletus

Suillus grevillei is found only under larch trees but then often in large numbers. **Edible**, but only after peeling away the sticky skin, after which they are best dried and used in soups or stews for flavour. **Cap** 3–11cm across, a lovely bright yellow colour but usually more orange in the button stage. Viscid. **Pores and tubes** lemon-yellow; pores small, bruising brownish. **Stem** has a floppy ring, sticky and marked orange below, yellow above. Season late summer to autumn.

Suillus aeruginascens is also found under larches, but is not common. The cap is whitish, creamy with dull buff markings; the pores are whitish-grey, the stem whitish-brown with a ring. **Edible.**

Suillus tridentinus is found only rarely, under larches. The cap is scaly, cracked, orange. The pores are orange and the stem yellowish-orange. **Edibility unknown.**

Hedgehog Fungus

Hedgehog Fungus photographed 7 October

Hedgehog Fungus

Hydnum repandum is an excellent edible mushroom that keeps well. It is commonly seen for sale in European markets. Remarkable in that it has spines in place of gills, thus giving rise to its common name Hedgehog Fungus. It is **edible** but the taste of the raw flesh is rather bitter and so it should always be cooked. Found in coniferous and broadleaved woods.

Cap 3–17cm across, velvety or suede-like, creamy-yellowish or flesh coloured. Spines 2–6mm long, whitish to salmon-pink. **Stem** often off-centre and lumpy at the base or two or three mushrooms amalgamating together. Creamy coloured, bruising yellowish-ochre near the base. Season late summer to late autumn.

INDEX

Roger Phillips has pioneered the photography of natural history which ensures reliable identification. By placing each specimen against a plain background he is able to show details that would otherwise have been lost if it had been photographed solely *in situ*. Such in the success of his technique that his books, which include the definitive guide to *Mushrooms* and *Wild Food*, have sold over a million copies worldwide. He is also the winner of numerous awards, including three for best produced and best designed books and the André Simon prize for 1983 for *Wild Food*.

Jacqui Hurst studied photography at Gloucestershire College of Art & Design, worked as an assistant to Roger Phillips for 4 years, and is now a freelance journalist and photographer, specialising in country matters.

The author and publishers believe the information contained in this book to be correct and accurate at the time of going to press. It is essential to be sure of the identification of a mushroom before cooking and eating it. If in doubt, don't. Neither the author nor the publishers can accept any legal responsibility or liability for any errors or omissions that may be made.

Acknowledgements

We should like to thank Alan Outen for the nine photographs he supplied and also Ted Green for his photograph and the enormous help he gave us in collecting. Jeff and Jenny Stone were also a great help in finding specimens.

HAMISH HAMILTON LTD

Published by the Penguin Group
Penguin Books Ltd, 27 Wrights Lane, London W8 5TZ, England
Penguin Books USA Inc., 375 Hudson Street, New York, New York, USA
Penguin Books Australia Ltd, Ringwood, Victoria, Australia
Penguin Books Canada Ltd, 10 Alcorn Avenue, Toronto, Ontario, Canada M4V3B2
Penguin Books (NZ) Ltd, 182-190 Wairau Road, Auckland 10, New Zealand

Penguin Books Ltd, Registered Offices: Harmondsworth, Middlesex, England

First published in Great Britain by Elm Tree Books/Hamish Hamilton Ltd 1986

Printed by Kyodo Printing Co (Singapore) Pte Ltd

A CIP catalogue record for this book is available from the British Library

ISBN 0-241-11811-5
ISBN 0-241-11756-9 Pbk